I Forgive You You Psycho!

An honest, 12-step program for getting over your toxic ex and living the life you were meant to live before they came in and f*cked it all up

KAT and STEWART

Copyright © 2023 by Kat and Stewart
All rights reserved. This book or any portion thereof may not be reproduced or used in
any manner whatsoever without the express written permission of the publisher except
for the use of brief quotations in a book review.

Publishing Services provided by Paper Raven Books LLC

Printed in the United States of America

First Printing, 2023

Paperback ISBN: 979-8-9894978-0-5

Disclaimer

Our attorneys, who we think are overly cautious but super cool, are making us tell you that these books are based on our personal histories and remedies that we discovered for ourselves and not psychological or medical advice for you, the reader.

I mean, we think we got this shit pretty well dialed in and we're crushing it right now, but hey… you do you. Legally.

Have you heard the story of ...

The Scorpion and the Frog?

One day a scorpion came to the side of a river. Needing to get across, the scorpion asked a frog at the bank of the river, "Frog, can you please let me ride on your back so I can get across the river?"

At first, terrified of the scorpion and then curious, the frog asked, "Why would I let you get on my back? You would only sting me!"

"Nonsense," replied the scorpion, "if I did that, then we both would die!"

The frog paused and thought about it and concluded that the scorpion was right and that he would give the scorpion a lift to the other side of the river.

Halfway across, the scorpion raised her tail and stung the frog, injecting her deadly poison into him.

"What have you done?" begged the frog, as he felt his body weaken. "Now we both are going to die! How could you do this?"

"I guess it's just my nature," replied the scorpion, as the two of them sank below the water.

Sound like someone you know?

Note to the frog:

"You own everything that happened to you. Tell your stories. If people wanted you to write warmly about them, they should have behaved better."
-Anne Lamott

"HOW DID I GET TO THIS INSANE POINT IN MY LIFE?"

Here's how… You gave the best of yourself to a vapid, shallow, black hole of a person because that was the best you thought you deserved. That black hole sucked you in until there was nothing left—not even your own light could escape.

You're reading this because you have suffered from your borderline partner's excessive abuse, manipulation, lies, shaming, control, gaslighting and selfishness. It's left you exhausted, defeated, resigned, and depressed—the very things the scorpion counts on.

This is the master tactic of the scorpion; to leave you so beaten down, small, and cut off from support that you simply give up and they can have their way, no matter the cost to you, your children, or anyone else in your orbit.

The worst of it is that they do an amazingly effective job of making it seem like *you're* the crazy one. That's their way of getting out of taking any responsibility for their abuse of you.

There's an old saying: "The healing can't begin until the gaslighting ends."

We've been there with our exes… we get it!

What we decided to do was to present a simple, 12-step recovery program for you to get you out from under the scorpion's sting and back to a place where you can thrive and be free from their poisonous effects.

Just like we did.

Be brave and bold, follow the 12 steps to recover from your toxic ex, and you'll finally be able to get back to the person you were before that fucking jerk messed it all up.

Step 1

ADMITTING YOU ASKED FOR THIS.

If this process is to work, you first need to admit that you were in a relationship with a narcissist, and you stayed with it far too long, hoping you could fix them.

But that doesn't take away the fact that they were a self-absorbed, egotistical, gaslighting, manipulative, abusive, demeaning, stupid fuck face.

I Forgive You, **YOU PSYCHO!**

Say this first part out loud:

- My fucking ex is a fucking psycho!
- They knew exactly what they were doing to me!
- They ruined my life and I fucking hate them!

Okay, good.

MANTRA FOR STEP 1:
THIS ONE'S ON ME.
Repeat after me:

- *I allowed it to happen.*
- *I am responsible for my choices.*
- *I have a lot of fucking work to do.*

Great! That's the first step. When in doubt, if you're starting to feel like a victim, repeat the first step.

Step 2:

BELIEVE THAT A CONCEPT GREATER THAN THE SCORPION'S INFLUENCE CAN GIVE YOU YOUR SELF-WORTH.

(Hint… it's YOU)

Recognize that you are not responsible for the scorpion's happiness. You can't fix them, no matter how much you try. It's time to focus on your own well-being.

And that starts with also owning the part you played in your own suffering.

I Forgive You, **YOU PSYCHO!**

Let's keep the real shit going:

- My ex is unfixable and doesn't want to change.
- I couldn't change them by loving them more.
- They played on my need to please, and put me in an un-winnable situation, where we both ignored my needs.

MANTRA FOR STEP 2:
FUCK. THEM.
Got it out of your system? Good.

Repeat after me:

- *I was convinced fixing the scorpion would give me value.*
- *I am responsible for my choices, not theirs.*
- *I have a shit ton of work to do.*
- *But I think I'm understanding what I've been missing here.*

Step 3

INVEST IN THERAPY OF SOME KIND.

Friends are great, but you can totally benefit from professional help. Your new 'fix' is you. Make a plan and begin to work on it.

Time for a real shift in thinking:

- I can't do this alone; I need to be honest about how I bent over and gave all my worth to some shithead so they could take a giant dookie all over it.
- Friends might have enabled me or at best given me distance to learn this on my own.
- I need to pay someone for the truth… therapy = honesty!

Let's do this!

MANTRA FOR STEP 3: **NOW ME, NEW ME.**

Repeat after me:

- *I needed to fix them, I needed to be needed. I needed to prove what I unconsciously thought about myself.*
- *I really do have a shit ton of work to do.*
- *But I don't have to do it alone. I'm going to find a therapist and commit to my mental health starting today.*

Step 4

TAKE A FIERCE LOOK IN THE MIRROR AND CLEAN UP YOUR SHIT.

What stupid things did you do while you were with this shit show of a person? Chances are they got you to distance yourself from friends and family. Welp, time to smack yourself in the head V8 style!

I Forgive You, **YOU PSYCHO!**

Time for a little real real:

- I let that insecure fucking psychopath talk me out of friends, family, career, etc.
- Shit!
- I admit that I did it to please them, and it cost me just about everything.

MANTRA FOR STEP 4:
I DON'T HATE YOU; I HATE WHO I BECAME BECAUSE OF YOU!

Action items:

- Make a list of the people you dismissed because of your scorpion's influence.
- Highlight with extreme honesty where you were hurtful or neglectful.
- FORGIVE YOURSELF.
- Go take a walk, get a drink, whatever clears your head. The next part involves some work.

Notes

Step 5

REMOVE ALL ITEMS OR REMINDERS OF YOUR VICTIMHOOD, NEED FOR VALIDATION, OR SELF-DOUBT.

Images are triggers, triggers are feelings, and feelings feel real when they're strong. You don't need this shit in your life. Get out the trash can.

Release!

- Trash the memories. Burn the letters. Rip up the pictures. Eliminate the triggers. Get rid of anything and everything that has the stank of the scorpion on it.
- While you're doing this, remember to practice self-compassion. Be kind to yourself and forgive yourself for any mistakes you may have made during the relationship.
- I let this person infiltrate every corner of my life and either shame it, ruin it, or destroy it. My home and surroundings will be a shrine to the new me!

MANTRA FOR STEP 5:
PURGE!
Tossed out all that toxic shit? Good.

Action Item:

- Create new spaces, put up new pictures, buy yourself that turtleneck you've always wanted!

Step 6

ADMITTING TO YOURSELF AND YOUR FAMILY FRIENDS AND CHILDREN WHERE YOU GOT OFF TRACK AND YOUR PLAN TO CORRECT IT.

Apologize to yourself for any self-doubt and self-blame that you experienced during the relationship. You were doing the best you could in an impossible situation.

But you know better now, and you can own up to it.

I Forgive You, YOU PSYCHO!

Suggested thoughts before eating that shit burger:

- My family and friends love me and will understand that I was manipulated.
- They will be glad that I have come out stronger, happier, and free.
- Some may be holding on to resentment—that's understandable.

MANTRA FOR STEP 6:
CLEAN UP YOUR MESS.
AFTER THAT, IT'S NONE OF YOUR BUSINESS WHAT ANYONE THINKS OF YOU.

ACTION ITEMS:

- Apologize to the people on your list. You first. Don't spend a lot of time on excuses, they'll get it. Just let them know you are committed to repairing the damage—however that looks and however long it takes.
- Their reaction is their reaction. You can't control it.
- Secretly curse your scorpion and imagine them being swarmed by murder hornets.
- Repeat.

Step 7

START TO LISTEN TO YOUR INSTINCTS AND TRUST THEM.

You know what's best for you, even if the scorpion tried to convince you otherwise.

I Forgive You, **YOU PSYCHO!**

New habits require effort:

- Catch yourself every time you dismiss your first thought for the one you think the scorpion would approve.
- You know what's right for you. You didn't honor it because you wanted to please the scorpion.

MANTRA FOR STEP 7:
LISTEN TO THE WHISPERS.
Can you hear them? That's your gut.

Action items:

- Do your best to side-step the old ways. Intuition is always quiet and you must begin listening for yours.
- You'll miss it a lot at first but don't stop trying. Eventually, you'll find your inner voice and it will roar!

Step 8

DON'T FORGET TO SEE THE RIDICULOUSNESS IN ALL OF THIS.

There's humor in wishing your ex get stampeded by a group of angry Walmart shoppers on coupon day!
    That's funny shit.

I Forgive You, **YOU PSYCHO!**

Remember yourself:

- Find joy in your playful imagination, laugh at how silly you were, and revel in your new life.

MANTRA FOR STEP 8:
FIND THE HUMOR IN ALL THINGS!
Healing requires humor!

Action items:

- Journal about every humorous thing you can think of relating to your new life without the scorpion, including how fun it was to dance around the ashes of old pictures.
- I mean, after all, they surely didn't look THAT good naked, right?

Step 9

RECONNECT WITH THOSE WHO ARE POSITIVE IN YOUR LIFE.

Surround yourself with supportive friends and family who understand what you went through and help you heal.

I Forgive You, **YOU PSYCHO!**

Take a look around:

- Funny thing about break-ups, you find out who your friends actually are. Sometimes, the ones you thought would stay scatter, and the ones you thought wouldn't care, show up for you.
- That shit happens.

MANTRA FOR STEP 9:
TEAM ME!
Reconnect with and build your 2.0 team.

Action items:

- Throw a party, welcoming your team.
- Share a drink, play cards, or a board game.
- Make sure they get home safe.
- Spend the rest of your life nurturing those people and allow yourself to be nurtured by them.

Step 10

LEARN TO CONTROL YOUR REACTIONS.

Think about what you endured. Scorpions love the sting. They love to drive you crazy. It's primarily so they can dismiss the shitty way they treated you by focusing solely on your reaction. That's super fucked up.

I Forgive You, **YOU PSYCHO!**

MANTRA FOR STEP 10: **RADIO SILENCE!**

If you have to interact with your ex, make sure it's plain, non-emotional, and factual.

As the old saying goes: "Never wrestle with a pig, you'll both get dirty but only one of you will like it."

They *will* try to bait you, so you need to be 100 percent bulletproof in this area.

Action items:

- Keep your eyes and ears sharp; you still may be easily pulled into the fight.
- Let yourself off the hook if you make a mistake, as you may make a few. Just learn from them and get better.
- Get SO good at not reacting to any past or possible scorpion in your life, you go from victim to victor!

Step 11

CREATE A HEALTHY ROUTINE, WHICH SUPPORTS YOUR EMERGING SELF-ESTEEM.

The goal at this point:

- Build your mind and body in such a way that you transform the person who allowed the scorpion to take over your life.
- Self-care doesn't just mean a good vibrator and a quart of Ben and Jerry's.

MANTRA FOR STEP 11:
MY EX MADE ME FEEL CRAZY, I DON'T HAVE TO PROVE THEM RIGHT.

Keep learning and growing. Read books, attend therapy, and educate yourself on narcissism recovery and choosing healthy relationships that don't suck ass.

Action Items:

- Seek out and join any group that supports activities that you love.
- Surround yourself with good music, etc.

OH… AND DO NOT DATE YET!!!

Step 12

BE A SHINING LIGHT FOR THOSE AROUND YOU.

MANTRA FOR STEP 12:
TEACH BY EXAMPLE.

And yes, that includes forgiving that fucking psycho coward bully who never had the courage to try any of this shit out for themselves.

Share your experience with others. You are not alone in your struggle with a narcissistic ex-partner. Be open about your journey and help others who may be going through the same thing.

The thing the Scorpion counts on the most is silence. You don't have to be silent. You're not the crazy one.

TRY TO IMAGINE YOUR SCORPION AS A LITTLE KID.

No one is *that* much of an asshole by choice. They were hurt early on and became the hurter. And they're a human, maybe even the co-parent of your children. That matters.

It's not easy, and it fucking sucks that you have to be the grown up, but here are some truths:

1. You chose a toxic person.

2. You did it for the wrong reasons, which you accept now.

3. You endured more suffering than a person has a right to.

4. You GOT OUT!

5. You decided to learn from your mistakes.

6. You grew.

That's a big fucking deal. So, forgive them, forgive yourself, and get out there and live your best life!

KAT AND STEWART'S FINAL THOUGHTS:

- Spread the word and be a warrior.
- Call out the scorpion loudly and often. They rely on silence to keep going.
- Recognize when you feel you 'have to' obey.
- Don't react. They feed off that and use your reaction as a way to distract from their own abuses.
- Be on guard. Always. And don't fall for niceness. It's not their nature to be kind and understanding. Empathy can easily be faked, and you know they use it as a tool.

When someone shows you who they are, believe it.

Let's be honest, what they did was unforgivable. After all, one of their primary talents is charm. That must come from somewhere. That could've been used for good to raise a happy family and to find peace, but they chose the other option. The point of this book is not letting them have a pass, but moving beyond it so you can have a life that you were meant to live, forgiving *yourself* for ever falling for that psycho!

DEFINITION OF TERMS

Gas-lighting
[gAS • layh-ting]

Okay, so let's say you look up into the sky and say, "I love that blue sky!" and your partner says—with great conviction, and in a shaming tone—it's not blue, it's orange. At first you question them, but they stick to their guns so strongly that eventually you start to believe it's you that is the crazy one. That's fucking gas-lighting. Watch the movie, "Gaslight", that's where the term originally comes from.

Manipulation
[muh-NIPP-yuh-LeY-shuhn]

The scorpion sees life as a series of battles and victories. Each issue that catches their attention must be fought over, so they set up the game in a way that baits you into either arguing with them (which causes a fight that they can then win, and you lose) or they have you so worried about whatever reaction they're going to have (anger, crying, guilt trip, etc.) that you simply give in before there's ever an issue.

Narcissist
[NAHR-suh-sist]

The narcissist is so broken, so damaged, and so void of any concern for anyone other than themselves, they set up their lives in a way where any failure, criticism, pushback, denial, or defense to their offense is considered an all-out assault on them. The world must do everything exactly as the narcissist wants or there will be hell to pay. In short, they are the worst kind of person because they have no interest in improving themselves or the world.

Stupid Fuck Face
[STOO-pid • FUHK-feyss]

Read the above. That fucker. Literally too stupid to be aware of anything outside of their own needs, wants, desires or inclinations. They have an opportunity—with you—to become better, to grow. Instead, they doubled down on their worst traits and sucked you under the water with them.

www.ingramcontent.com/pod-product-compliance
Lightning Source LLC
Chambersburg PA
CBHW051618010526
44119CB00008B/189